G000097375

SPA MAMA

SPA MAMA
Pampering for the Mother-to-Be

by Stacy Denney

Foreword by Susan Lawler, R.N.
Illustrations by Kerrie Hess

CHRONICLE BOOKS
SAN FRANCISCO

Text copyright © 2005 by Stacy Denney.

Illustrations copyright © 2005 by Kerrie Hess.

Library of Congress Cataloging-in-Publication Data available.

ISBN 0-8118-4884-1

Manufactured in China.

Design by Aesthetic Apparatus

Distributed in Canada by Raincoast Books
9050 Shaughnessy Street
Vancouver, British Columbia V6P 6E5

10 9 8 7 6 5 4 3 2 1

Chronicle Books LLC
85 Second Street
San Francisco, California 94105

www.chroniclebooks.com

Notice: The authors have done their best in preparing this book, but make no representations or
warranties with respect to the accuracy or completeness of the contents. The authors and publisher
disclaim any liability from any injury that may result from the use, proper or improper, of the
information contained in this book. The accuracy and completeness of the information provided
herein and the opinions stated herein are not guaranteed or warranted to produce any particular
results, and the advice and strategies contained herein may not be suitable for every individual.
The information is not intended to substitute for the knowledge and advice of your own health-
care provider and your own common sense. Whenever you have concerns or questions about your
health or the health of your child, consult your doctor or other health-care professional. Always
consult with your physician before using any of the suggestions outlined in this guidebook.

CONTENTS

Foreword by Susan Lawler, R.N.
Page 10

Introduction
Page 12

THE FIRST TRIMESTER

What to Eat When You Can't
Snacking your way through first-trimester nausea • Page 17

Baby Your Face
Relaxing facial massage • Page 18

Staying Fit in the First Trimester
What do you mean, my pelvis has a floor? • Page 20

Water, Water, and More Water
A high five for hydration • Page 22

Scrub-A-Dub-Dub
Invigorating sugar body scrub • Page 24

Ginger Tea
The anti-nausea pick-me-up • Page 26

Berry Refreshing
Wake-up cleanser for normal skin • Page 28

Sweet and Simple Facial Mask
Bye-bye break-outs • Page 30

The Ancient Art of Acupressure
And other nausea-relieving strategies • Page 32

Bananas in Coconut Milk
Simple flavors for a delicate stomach • Page 34

Golf-Ball Foot Massage
Hit nausea with a hole-in-one • Page 36

Lullaby Time
Moisturizing night cream for normal skin • Page 38

Prenatal Supplements
Why eating for two isn't always enough • Page 40

Folic-Acid Foods
Natural nutrition for a healthy baby • Page 42

Yoga for the First Trimester
The Downward Dog • Page 44

THE SECOND TRIMESTER

Lavender Bubble Bath
Soothe and heal your body • Page 49

Yoga for the Second Trimester
The Butterfly • Page 50

Anyone for Tennis?
The sport never felt so good • Page 52

Oh, the Decadence!
Yummy chocolate mask for normal skin • Page 53

Getting Your Head Around the Weight Gain
Or, I'm having a baby,
so how come my butt's getting bigger? • Page 54

Chardonnay Clarifying Mask
Overnight mask for oily skin • Page 56

C You Later, Acne
A wake-up call for unruly skin • Page 57

Buddha Belly Mask
Soothe your growing belly • Page 58

Too Much Baby, Not Enough Lung
How to cope with compromised breathing • Page 60

Salmon with Lemon Pesto
A healthy feast for you and your baby • Page 62

Iced Berry Lemonade
A nutrient-packed zinger • Page 64

Avoiding Stretch Marks
You can run, but you can't hide • Page 65

Staying Fit in the Second Trimester
Enjoying your new-found energy • Page 66

It's a Revelation
Get behind the mask of pregnancy • Page 68

Rosewater Facial Cocktail
Clarifying toner for acne-prone skin • Page 69

THE THIRD TRIMESTER

Strawberry Smoothie
A protein-packed fruit punch • Page 73

Barefoot & Pregnant Belly Cast
Preserve your belly in all its glory • Page 74

Smart Sleeping Positions
How to get a good night's rest (before it's too late) • Page 76

Rise and Shine
Oatmeal mask for dry skin • Page 78

Staying Fit in the Third Trimester
The great pregnancy balancing act • Page 80

Fresh and Fruity
Citrus mask for oily skin • Page 82

Asian Cabbage Crunch Salad
The healthiest way to get your greens • Page 84

Just Juice
Counterpressure of the fruity kind • Page 86

Yoga for the Third Trimester
Deep squatting, or the Garland • Page 88

Hand 'Em Over
Be kind to your carpal tunnel • Page 90

Fresh Cheeks Toner
For a calming effect • Page 92

Coping with Cankles
When it's not just your belly that's getting bigger • Page 93

Simply Sciatic
Quick relief for a pain in the butt • Page 94

Sweet Potato Potion
Intense nighttime moisturizing for oil-prone skin • Page 96

Perineal Massage
Make room for baby • Page 97

Baby Shower Etiquette for the Mom-to-Be
Or, how to get what you really want • Page 98

Your In-Home Full-Body Massage
Down with fatigue, up with energy • Page 100

What to Take to the Hospital
Staying cute while contracting • Page 102

NOW YOU ARE TWO

Yummy Pec Stretch
Work a little muscle-strain magic • Page 107

Looking Good for the First Photos
(Even though you were in labor for thirty-six hours) • Page 108

Mother's Little Helper
Soothing shoulder, neck, and head massage • Page 110

Baby Foot and Leg Massage
Pure relaxation for both of you • Page 112

Sleepless in [insert home town here]
Survival tactics for the new mom • Page 114

There's a Baby in Your Spa
Why the pampering doesn't have to end • Page 116

Acknowledgments • Page 119

FOREWORD

Pregnancy is a celebration of motherhood and new life. It is one of nature's finest accomplishments and a time in a woman's life that deserves respect. Gone are the days when women were confined during their pregnancy, shrouded in fear and mystery. It's time to reclaim the ancient wisdom of motherhood. Honoring this miracle and nurturing the women who create it are what this book is all about.

Pregnancy is a wonderful time to pamper yourself with body and facial treatments. Both can enhance feelings of well-being, support normal physiological adaptations, and alleviate many of the discomforts common during pregnancy. If you are experiencing a normal pregnancy and are under the care of a physician or certified nurse midwife, you need take only a few precautions to safely enjoy your at-home spa experience.

In general, be sure to stay hydrated, use the bathroom frequently, and change position as often as you need to. If any treatment causes discomfort, be sensible and stop. Always sample the feel and scent of a product before using it, as a pregnant woman's senses are often more acute. You may find that usually benign scents are now overwhelming.

Very few treatments are specifically contraindicated. Facials are wonderful for enhancing the glow of pregnancy, although you should avoid facial peels and microdermabrasion because of the facial-skin sensitivity and hyper-pigmentation that goes along with pregnancy. Massages can do much to reduce discomforts such as backache, shoulder and neck strain, and edema. If your partner or a friend is giving you a treatment, he or she should always use a light hand, as many women are more sensitive to touch during pregnancy due to the increase in blood volume and blood vessels.

If you use essential oils, please take a conservative approach. Never apply essential oils directly to the skin, and never take them internally. They should always be diluted in a neutral base oil. That said, many essential oils can be very restorative during pregnancy when used in massages, baths, and facials. Lavender is a particularly popular oil that can help soothe aches and pains, as well as aiding relaxation and lifting depression. When pregnant, however, you should avoid the stronger, more stimulating oils such as peppermint, camphor, and juniper. If in doubt, err on the side of caution.

As more studies are completed, data suggests the best guidelines for a pregnant woman planning spa treatments should come from herself. That is, listen to your body. If something doesn't feel comfortable, don't do it. If it does feel comfortable, enjoy!

—Susan Lawler, R.N.

INTRODUCTION

When I first found out I was pregnant, I felt the usual rush of emotions: joy, excitement, a little bit of fear, and, of course, absolute euphoria that I now had an iron-clad excuse to indulge myself completely, and without shame. And for me, that meant even more spa days.

Fortunately, I was in the right business. Back in October 2003, a long-held dream of mine had finally come to fruition with the opening of my spa, Barefoot & Pregnant, a place dedicated to nurturing pregnant women as they journeyed to motherhood. Along with prenatal exercise classes, childbirth and parenting workshops, and support groups, I had also made space for a fabulous day spa offering treatments created specifically for pregnant women: facials for hormonally challenged skin and massages to ease all those new aches and pains.

Having witnessed a number of very good friends struggle through their pregnancies, giving themselves mind, body, and soul to nurturing their babies-to-be while neglecting their own emotional and physical needs, I knew that Barefoot & Pregnant had an important role to play. However, it was only when I became pregnant myself, (somewhat later than my contemporaries), that I realized what a great place it actually was (if I say so myself).

While I mustered enough energy for a weekly exercise class or two and signed up for childbirth classes, I took particular advantage of the spa. Draped in a towel, submerged in soothing music, I felt the aches of pregnancy (my back, my legs, my shoulders), along with the anxieties (What if my child is ugly? What if I turn out to be an unfit mother? What if my ankles never return to an acceptable circumference?) simply melt away.

Spa aficionados know that there are few things more conducive to brilliant thinking than being thoroughly relaxed. So, as I struggled, while enjoying a very lovely foot massage, with the desire to welcome all pregnant women everywhere to Barefoot & Pregnant (clearly an impractical notion), I had a flash of insight (unusual, I know, in the first trimester). I realized how I could make it easier for pregnant women to pamper themselves: I could simply write it all down in a book.

And so I did. And here it is. From head to foot, belly to back, within these pages you'll find a bunch of simple recipes for prenatal treatments: facials, massages, masks, and more. Each has been formulated to give you all the mental and physical benefits of a luxurious spa treatment without the inconvenience of actually having to leave your home. And the more pregnant you become, I can assure you, the more appealing that particular notion will be.

I've also thrown in (because I just can't help myself) a few pages of my own wisdom (speaking as a former pregnant person and self-confessed hedonist) on staying happy and healthy while having a baby. So get comfortable, relax, and make the most of the perfect opportunity to pamper yourself.

THE FIRST TRIMESTER

Congratulations. You're pregnant.

A baby about the size of your pinkie nail (or the width of your newly manicured hand if you're a little further on and quite well put together) is currently having a very pleasant time of it in your belly.

He or she is eating, growing, and generally enjoying the lap pool that is your amniotic sac. You, however, may not be feeling quite so perky. Which is why this really is the time to start pampering yourself. And, let's face it, unless you've told people why you're eating unbuttered toast for breakfast or spending an unseemly amount of time in the bathroom, nobody else is going to start spoiling you.

To start you off on your glorious nine-month journey of self-nurturing, here's a collection of simple recipes for your home spa experience, interspersed with my own personal strategies for coping with the early stages of pregnancy. On each and every page, you'll find something to quash the nausea and banish the fatigue, while putting a glow in your cheeks and a spring in your step.

So, congratulations again. And let the self-indulgence begin.

WHAT TO EAT WHEN YOU CAN'T

Snacking your way through first-trimester nausea

If, like me, you spend more time in the bathroom than the kitchen during the first few months of pregnancy, you are probably dogged by the world's most inaccurately named condition: morning sickness.

Whatever time of day (or night) it strikes, know that the nausea usually passes by week 16 or so, and you will go on to eat your entire body weight in chocolate brownies before your baby is born. For now, here are some foods that may make you feel a little better (or, at least, a little less nauseous).

Ginger: Fresh, pickled, candied, in a tea bag, or as a capsule. Whatever the format, ginger is a natural remedy for nausea.

Crackers: An old stand-by, but effective for many women. Likewise *potato chips* (they're saltier, not necessarily a good thing, but you'll leave fewer crumbs in your wake, which is useful as vacuuming probably isn't high on your to-do list right now). Some women swear by *rice cakes*.

Frozen yogurt: It looks like ice cream. It even tastes a little like ice cream. And it's pretty gentle on your stomach. Plus, you don't have to do all that nausea-inducing chewing and swallowing. Same goes for *applesauce*, *oatmeal*, and *pudding*.

Lemons: Simply sniff a cut lemon to relieve nausea.

BABY YOUR FACE

Relaxing facial massage

This is a great way to relieve headache or sinus pain. All you need are your own two hands and a comfortable place to sit or lie down.

Forehead: Using the fingertips of both hands, stroke your forehead from the midpoint toward the temple as if you were drawing 4 rows between your brow and your hairline.

Eyebrow ridge: With both hands poised above the bridge of your nose, inhale deeply. Pinch your eyebrow ridge as you exhale. Inhale and move your fingers to a new position along the ridge. Exhale as you pinch, and so on.

Nose and cheekbones: Using both hands, draw your middle and index fingers down either side of your nose, pausing where cheekbone meets nostril. Inhale and press your fingers toward the back of your head. Continue tracing underneath your cheekbone until you reach your temples.

Jawbone: Make small circles with your fingertips from the temple down along the jawbone to the tip of the chin.

Cheeks: With your hands in a loose fist, use the flat part of your fingers to make circles in the fleshy part of your cheeks.

Ears: Pinch the edge of your ears from the top ridge down to the lobe and back, gently pulling as you do so.

Head: With flat fingers, push up from the corner of your jawbone to your temple. Continue up and over your ears and down along the underside of your jawbone, finishing under the tip of your chin. Then, massage your whole head with your fingertips as if you were shampooing.

STAYING FIT IN THE FIRST TRIMESTER

What do you mean, my pelvis has a floor?

If you've reined in the temptation to skip this page, I commend you. Exercise during pregnancy may seem to be a concept that flies in the face of every self-respecting, ice-cream-eating pregnant woman, but nine months from now you'll be glad you got off your backside once in a while.

Beginning an exercise program: If you don't currently exercise on a regular basis, now is the perfect time to start. Find yourself an exercise facility or personal trainer with experience in prenatal fitness, and keep your doctor or midwife in the loop on your new activity.

Continuing an exercise program: If you already exercise regularly, you can continue to do so throughout your pregnancy, with only a few modifications. Try brisk walking instead of running, for example, as it's easier on your changing body. The general rule of thumb is that if you can't carry on a conversation while working out, slow down.

Your pelvic floor: This refers to the sling of muscles that forms the base of your pelvis. And a well-toned set can make for an easier, less painful (or more accurately, a slightly less difficult and slightly less painful) birth. Regular *Kegel exercises* can work wonders: Simply tighten your pelvic floor muscles (imagine you are trying to stop peeing halfway through a trip to the bathroom), hold for 5 seconds, and then release. Start with 10 repetitions, 4 times a day.

Whatever you do to keep fit, stay well hydrated and avoid becoming overheated or fatigued: This is so important that I'll be saying it again. And again.

WATER, WATER, AND MORE WATER
A high five for hydration

When you're pregnant, you need 64 fluid ounces a day to keep you and your baby well hydrated. That's a lot of liquid, and sadly, eight decaf vanilla lattes just aren't going to cut it. From this point on, water (not juice, not herbal tea) has to be your beverage of choice. Read on to learn why you need more than ever before.

Your amniotic sac: Help the little guy or gal stay afloat. Amniotic fluid replenishes itself every day, and it's got to come from somewhere.

Your bowels: More water means less constipation. Need I say more?

Your kidneys: Extra fluids help your hard-working kidneys function better, while warding off urinary tract infections.

Your skin: As every self-respecting aficionado of women's magazines knows, water is great for your skin. So if you're a little at odds with how your body is changing, a glowing complexion is an excellent way to divert attention away from your magnificent new chest.

Your baby: Later on in your pregnancy, dehydration can cause contractions that can lead to premature delivery.

So, more water's a good thing. But if, pre-pregnancy, your daily glass was typically the one you chugged just before bed in a futile attempt to stave off a hangover, then you may find upping your intake to eight 8-ounce glasses a day quite the task.

My advice: Carry a water-filled sports bottle everywhere you go. As well as helping you stay well hydrated, it will also foster the illusion that, despite appearances to the contrary, you've just run a terribly exhilarating 10K.

SCRUB-A-DUB-DUB
Invigorating sugar body scrub

It's generally presumed (although not medically proven) that taking hot baths in the first trimester can be harmful to the developing fetus. If you're erring on the side of caution and consequently foregoing those long, luxurious soaks, then this total-body scrub will remind you of the good old days (you have to climb in the tub to do it, and you'll emerge smelling fabulous).

This scrub also helps to improve circulation, which is useful, as by the end of your first trimester your poor heart will be working twice as hard as usual, pumping more than seven quarts of blood a minute to keep you and your baby healthy.

Depending on how big you and your belly are getting, the recipe makes enough for 1 or 2 applications. If there's any left over after your first total-body scrubbing experience, simply store it in the fridge.

Makes 1 to 2 applications

³/₄ cup brown sugar
¹/₂ tablespoon honey
¹/₄ cup jojoba oil
¹/₈ cup liquid soap

In a medium bowl, combine all the ingredients and stir to mix them thoroughly. Make sure your bathroom is warm. Dry the tub, add a bath mat, line the bottom of the tub with towels, and lower yourself in. Gently massage the scrub all over your skin from neck to toe (it's a little too abrasive for your face). After a full-body application, remove the towels from the tub and rinse the scrub from your skin with warm water. The jojoba oil will make the tub slippery, so be very careful when rinsing yourself, and when getting out.

GINGER TEA

The anti-nausea pick-me-up

It's impossible to be pregnant without hearing about morning sickness. And it's impossible for you to hear about morning sickness without hearing people extol the virtues of ginger as a natural and effective remedy. They're right, too. Ginger in many different forms is a proven way of combating nausea: The grated fresh ginger used here aids digestion and helps settle a tempestuous tummy. Raspberry leaves have long been used as a detoxificant, and Rapadura is the most natural form of sugar commercially available; if you can't find it in your local health food emporium, use honey instead.

This tea also makes a great cold ginger ale. Simply add your sweetener of choice and chill before mixing with sparkling water and serving with lemon slices.

Makes 8 cups

8 cups water
2 teaspoons grated fresh ginger
2 bay leaves
$1/2$ teaspoon dried red raspberry leaves
$1/2$ tablespoon Rapadura, plus more to taste

In a large saucepan, combine the water, ginger, bay leaves, raspberry leaves, and the ½ tablespoon Rapadura. Bring to a boil, reduce heat, and simmer for 5 minutes. Drain and serve hot with more Rapadura to taste. You can store the tea in a sealed container in the refrigerator for about a week, reheating only as much as you need each time.

BERRY REFRESHING
Wake-up cleanser for normal skin

This super-refreshing fruity cleanser is the perfect *good-morning-honey-I'm-wide-awake-and-raring-to-go (before-I-flop-down-on-the-sofa-with-a-decaf-latte)* way to start the day. Blackberries contain alpha hydroxy acid, a natural exfoliant that helps to remove dead skin cells and regenerate new ones. And best of all (because growing a baby is making you more than a little tired), it takes only about 45 seconds to concoct.

As this recipe calls for just 6 blackberries (and it's virtually impossible to buy just 6 blackberries), it's likely that you'll have some left over. When you've made the cleanser, wash the blender and whip up a delicious breakfast smoothie using natural yogurt and the rest of the blackberries.

Makes 1 to 2 applications
6 ripe blackberries
2 teaspoons almond oil
1 tablespoon witch hazel

In a blender, combine all the ingredients and blend until smooth. Spread the mixture on your face, massaging it lightly into the skin. Rinse off with warm water, then splash your face with cool water for a really exhilarating effect. This recipe makes between 1 and 2 applications, depending on how much cleanser you typically like to use. As there are no preservatives in this concoction, please store it in the refrigerator and be sure to use it all within about 5 days.

SWEET AND SIMPLE FACIAL MASK

Bye-bye break-outs

What a strange thing pregnancy is. Here you are, on the brink of the single most maturing event of your life, and your face is breaking out like that of a thirteen-year-old.

Although it doesn't happen to all women, acne is a fairly common by-product of those pregnancy hormones, and it usually strikes in the first trimester. And of course, being pregnant, your skin-care options are rather limited. Abrasive scrubs and exfoliants may enrage your newly sensitive skin, and the anti-acne prescription drugs Accutane and Retin-A are absolute no-nos during pregnancy. Instead, try this natural and gentle facial mask designed to unplug your oily pores without irritating your skin. Remember that facial masks should be used no more than once or twice a week.

Makes 1 application

2 tablespoons bran
1 tablespoon baby applesauce
1 tablespoon fresh lemon juice
1 teaspoon dried peppermint

In a small bowl, combine all the ingredients and stir to make a paste. Spread the gooey mixture on your face. Treat yourself to a quick 20-minute nap, then rinse the mask off with lukewarm water.

THE ANCIENT ART OF ACUPRESSURE

And other nausea-relieving strategies

There are all kinds of tricks to reduce nausea out there, some more effective than others. But if you're subsisting on a diet of dry crackers, peppermint tea, and candied ginger and you still feel terrible, maybe it's time to try something new.

The traditional Chinese technique of acupressure has been shown to relieve nausea and vomiting in some pregnant women. It's easy to do and perfectly safe. Here's how: Using the tip of your thumb, press on the inside of your arm, about 3 fingers' width from your wrist crease. If it feels a little tender you've found the spot. Hold this pressure for a count of 10, then rest for a count of 10. Do this 6 times, or simply maintain the pressure until your nausea starts to subside.

Depending on the severity of your morning sickness, you might also consider the options below.

Acupuncture: This therapy operates on the same principle as acupressure, although as it uses needles it's more invasive. Studies have shown that acupuncture can relieve or reduce the symptoms of *hyperemesis gravidarum* (severe pregnancy vomiting that leads to dehydration and requires hospitalization) in some women.

Extra vitamin B$_6$: 50 milligrams of vitamin B$_6$ twice a day has been shown to relieve nausea. You can buy this at your local natural-foods store or pharmacy, but talk to your doctor before self-prescribing.

BANANAS IN COCONUT MILK

Simple flavors for a delicate stomach

Morning sickness is caused by the hormones that support your pregnancy, so feeling constantly nauseated is actually a good thing (in a really bad, stomach-churning way). Nevertheless, wobbly first-trimester tummies need special treatment. Try this comforting banana dessert, which supplies great nutrition for both you and your resident fetus.

The potassium in the bananas can help alleviate some of your body's aches and pains (even that associated with leg waxing, should you be approaching pregnancy with every intention of staying glamorous and stubble-free), while the coconut milk works to build body mass for your baby. This recipe also uses maple syrup, which is so much better for you than sugar, and flaxseed, which is full of essential fatty acids. The flaxseed also helps with that other delightful digestive symptom of pregnancy, constipation.

Makes 2 servings

2 ripe bananas
1/2 can coconut milk
1/4 cup water
1/4 cup maple syrup
1/2 teaspoon salt
1/2 tablespoon flaxseed

Peel the bananas and cut each into 1-inch segments. In a medium saucepan, combine the coconut milk, water, and maple syrup. Place over medium-low heat and bring to a simmer. Add the sliced bananas and simmer for 10 minutes. Finally, add the salt, increase the heat to medium-high, and boil for 20 minutes to reduce the mixture to a puddinglike consistency. The bananas will fall apart, or you can mash them further if you like. Serve topped with flaxseed. You can keep any leftovers (unlikely) in the refrigerator for up to 1 week.

GOLF-BALL FOOT MASSAGE
Hit nausea with a hole-in-one

Golf-ball foot massage. It sounds so hearty and active.
Fortunately, nothing could be further from the truth. This
great treatment starts off with a wonderfully fragrant foot
soak containing mandarin essential oil, known to relieve all
kinds of stomach upsets, including morning sickness. And
rolling your foot over a golf ball will pep up even the most
tired of toes.

You can purchase golf balls quite cheaply at your local
sporting goods store, a quick foray into which may make you
heartily glad that pregnancy allows you to eschew all that
unnecessary athleticism.

You will need:
Mandarin or tangerine essential oil
A large, deep bowl big enough for your feet side by side
2 towels
2 golf balls

Put 6 drops of the essential oil in the bowl and fill it with warm water. Put the bowl on the floor in front of a comfy chair, with a towel on either side and a golf ball on each towel. Soak your feet for a few minutes. Take your left foot out and roll the golf ball over the towel using the arch of your foot. Then, switch feet. Add more warm water to the bowl as it cools.

If you're suffering from more extreme nausea, use spearmint essential oil instead of mandarin or tangerine. (I don't recommend that you use peppermint essential oil during pregnancy, as it's too intense.)

Remember, essential oils are powerful substances, so treat them with respect, especially when you're having a baby. They should always be diluted, never be applied directly to the skin, and never be ingested.

Moisturizing night cream for normal skin

During the first trimester, pregnant women sleep (or try to sleep) an inordinate amount of time. Most nights, you'll probably be in your jammies on the sofa by 7 P.M. and tucked up in bed an hour later. Good-bye social life; hello cozy comforter. Luckily, the more you sleep, the more benefit you'll get from this great nighttime potion.

Use this combination of apple juice, glycerin, and sweet almond oil every evening and you'll wake up with glowing, healthy skin. Apple juice works wonders on fine wrinkles and cracked skin, while the sweet almond oil combats dryness and reduces the appearance of scarring and the skin imperfections that can occur during pregnancy.

This recipe makes enough for about 7 nighttime applications. As it's all natural and preservative-free, you should discard any that you do not use within a week.

Makes about 7 applications
1 tablespoon apple juice
1 teaspoon glycerin
1 tablespoon sweet almond oil

In a small saucepan, mix all the ingredients over a low heat until thoroughly combined. Transfer the cream to a small, sterile plastic container. To use, massage a few drops onto your freshly cleansed skin before going to sleep.

PRENATAL SUPPLEMENTS

Why eating for two isn't always enough

You eat three healthful meals a day. You snack on raw vegetables. You can spot a high-protein, low-fat entrée at thirty paces. Why, then, does your doctor tell you to take a daily prenatal vitamin and mineral supplement? Read on.

Folic acid: This B vitamin is absolutely essential for the healthy development of your baby. Because your body actually utilizes the folic acid in supplements better than that contained naturally in foods, you should take a prenatal vitamin tablet containing *400 to 800 micrograms each and every day*. Kudos to you if you started taking folic acid *before* you got pregnant. If not, start taking it now and keep taking it.

Iron: Being pregnant and iron-deficient is a bad combination. You'll feel tired and irritable, and you may be at risk of delivering prematurely. Unfortunately, even a hard-core carnivore will have trouble getting enough iron through diet alone. Take a supplement that gives you *60 milligrams a day*, and remember that caffeine decreases your body's ability to absorb iron, while foods high in vitamin C increase it. A great excuse, should you need one, for a spinach and strawberry smoothie.

Calcium: If you don't take in enough calcium to build healthy bones for your baby, your devious little fetus will actually pull calcium from *your* bones, putting you at risk for osteoporosis later in life. For once, it's easy to get the recommended *1,600 milligrams a day* from your diet. A cup of milk on your (iron-fortified) breakfast cereal, a large yogurt smoothie for your midmorning snack, and you're halfway there.

FOLIC-ACID FOODS

Natural nutrition for a healthy baby

The easiest way to get enough folic acid is by remembering to take your prenatal vitamins every day. But what if you're one of the many pregnant women who can't stomach prenatal supplements, especially in the first trimester?

Here are some simple (and gentle) ways to up your folic acid intake without bringing your digestive equilibrium down.

Fortified breakfast cereals: There couldn't be an easier way to get more folic acid in your diet. Add skim milk and you have a meal that's low in fat and high in calcium too.

Wheat germ: If all you can stomach is dry toast, make sure it's whole-grain.

Legumes: Chickpeas, kidney beans, soy beans, and the like. Make a soup or throw them in a salad. They're very versatile and very good for you.

Oranges and orange juice: As well as being a good source of folic acid, orange juice helps your body absorb iron and can also relieve constipation.

Walnuts, almonds, and peanuts: Snack on a handful or two, or double up on the good stuff by making yourself a peanut butter sandwich with whole-grain bread.

Vegetables: Dark green leafy vegetables like broccoli and spinach, as well as asparagus, Brussels sprouts, and green beans, are good natural sources of folic acid. Lightly steam your veggie of choice and serve it as a side dish if you can't face a whole plateful.

While it's possible to include a wide variety of folic-acid foods in your diet, the folic acid contained in prenatal supplements is more easily metabolized by your body. Talk to your doctor before discarding your prenatal vitamins, as he or she may be able to prescribe a formulation that your tummy finds more tolerable.

YOGA FOR THE FIRST TRIMESTER
The Downward Dog

Yoga is respectful of both your rapidly changing body *and* your increasingly anxious mind. This pose in particular is perfect for the first trimester. It helps to alleviate physical and mental fatigue, while increasing hip flexibility (which, a few months from now, you'll be very glad to have).

1. Start on your hands and knees. Your knees should be hip-width apart, with your feet directly behind the knees and your palms directly under your shoulders, with your fingers facing forward. Look down between your hands so that your back is flat.

2. With straight arms, lift your hips toward the ceiling. Keep your spine as straight and long as possible and let your head hang loosely.

3. Spread your fingers wide apart with the middle finger facing forward and the palms shoulder-width apart. Press your fingers and palms into the floor.

4. Your feet should still be hip-width apart, with your toes facing forward. Press your heels into the floor so that you feel a stretch in the back of your legs. Keep your legs straight or slightly bent.

5. Breathe deeply and hold for up to 2 minutes.

Later on, when you're a little bigger, you'll find the Downward Dog a great way to relieve lower-back pain and late-night leg cramps. And if the weight of your small but solid baby right on your bladder keeps you awake, try doing this pose with your legs bent.

THE SECOND TRIMESTER

Congratulations. You're showing.

Now they all get why you've been beset by lethargy, anxiety, and strange eating habits (a particularly antisocial combination). But with the second trimester in full swing, all that's behind you. You feel amazing. You exude vitality. You're bursting with energy (at least when you're sitting down). And joy of joys, after years of crunching your abs and holding your stomach in, you are now free to have a belly.

This trimester you'll start to feel your baby move (not to be mistaken for gas). You'll rediscover the joy of eating a meal not created entirely out of crackers. You can start wearing those cute maternity clothes. And you can legitimately buy things for your future offspring.

With all this eating, shopping, and, oh yes, being pregnant, you're probably in need of a little nurturing. Read on for treatments designed to ease the aches and pains that develop as your baby grows, stretching your body in all kinds of new and interesting ways. There are masks and massages, bubble baths and belly treatments, all topped off with a few thoughts on staying physically fit and emotionally stable even as your midsection expands like a thing possessed.

LAVENDER BUBBLE BATH
Soothe and heal your body

In just a few short months, the precious time you currently spend luxuriating in the bathtub will have been commandeered by a small, slippery infant with cleansing demands of his or her own. So, it's only sensible to really make the most of the bath-time opportunities that remain before you give birth. Try this lavender bubble bath with pleasantly warm (not hot) water. Lavender oil is noted for its soothing properties and is particularly beneficial for aching backs, legs and ligaments, so it's luxurious and decadent in an absolutely-essential-for-a-pregnant-woman way.

Makes about 4 ½ cups

4 cups water
1 bar of your favorite unscented soap, grated
¼ cup coconut oil
3 drops lavender essential oil

In a medium saucepan, warm the water over low heat. Add the soap and stir until dissolved. Remove the pan from the heat and add the coconut and lavender oils. Draw yourself a nice deep bath, add at least a cup of your newly concocted bubble bath, and enjoy. You can store the remainder in a sealed jar, in the refrigerator for up to 1 week.

YOGA FOR THE SECOND TRIMESTER

The Butterfly

Sciatica. It's a pain in the butt. There's no other way to describe it, because that's exactly what it is. (For the technically minded, sciatica is caused when either your pelvic joint, the baby's head, or your growing uterus puts pressure on the sciatic nerve in your lower back.)

Not for the first time, it's yoga to the rescue. If your backside is causing you unusual but severe pain, try doing the Butterfly several times a day.

1. Sit on the floor with your spine straight. Bring the soles of your feet, heels together, toward your groin so that your knees fall apart.

2. Lean forward to place your hands on the floor in front of you, or hold onto your ankles.

3. In this position, practice lifting your pelvic floor (that part of your anatomy with which you are now, no doubt, intimately acquainted, seeing as you do your Kegel exercises so often).

4. Then, draw in your belly as much as you can (or at least try to). This will make your spine even longer, and create more space for you and your baby.

5. Spread your legs (sorry, there's no other way to put it) as wide as possible, pushing your knees toward the floor. Relax your groin, and allow your hips to open.

6. Hold this position for up to 1 minute. Release by sitting up, keeping your spine straight.

ANYONE FOR TENNIS?
The sport never felt so good

When you spend your days asking your feet to bear an increasingly heavy load, it's always nice to reward them with a nice foot rub at the end of an evening. Until, of course, you can no longer reach them. This clever massage uses tennis balls so you can ease your feet (and other parts of your body) without lifting a finger.

Foot massage: Stand barefoot near a wall or holding onto a chair. Put one foot on top of a tennis ball placed on the floor and lean your weight onto it, rolling the arch of your foot back and forth slowly.

Bottom massage: Place a tennis ball between the wall and one of your butt cheeks and lean into it. Roll the ball all around your overworked gluteal muscles by bending and extending your knees. Repeat on the other side.

Back massage: Bend your knees and place the ball between the edge of one shoulder blade and your spine. Press into the wall, then bend and extend your knees to roll the ball around your upper back. Move the ball down until you find the squarish muscle that connects your lowest rib to the top ridge of the hipbone. Then, press into the wall and roll the ball around.

OH, THE DECADENCE!

Yummy chocolate mask for normal skin

While you may have sworn off the cocktails, and (I trust) given cigarettes and secondhand smoke an extremely wide berth, chocolate in all its forms and flavors is a minor vice that's very much tolerated by the pregnancy police.

But if your daily ritual of baking chocolate chip cookies with a cup of hot cocoa at your elbow and a bowl of M&Ms within reach isn't enough of a fix, you can now give your addiction free rein with this wonderfully indulgent, deliciously aromatic chocolate facial mask.

Next to the whole chocolate-on-your-face thing you may not even care, but the combination of cocoa powder and cream really can refresh a tired complexion. Exactly why, I couldn't tell you. I guess it's all down to the magic of chocolate.

Makes 1 application
1 tablespoon rolled oats
⅓ cup unsweetened cocoa powder
3 tablespoons heavy cream
2 teaspoons cottage cheese
1 tablespoon avocado
½ cup honey

In a blender, grind the oats to a fine powder. In a small bowl, combine the oats and all the remaining ingredients and stir to blend. Spread all of the mixture over your face. Relax for 10 minutes, then wash the mask off with warm water (or, if pregnancy has given you a taste for obscure food combinations, simply lick it off).

GETTING YOUR HEAD AROUND THE WEIGHT GAIN

Or, I'm having a baby, so how come my butt's getting bigger?

You've probably been told that the average woman gains between twenty-five and thirty-five pounds throughout the course of her pregnancy. But averages are, as we all know, things that happen to other people. Larger women tend to gain less, smaller women more, and Hollywood celebrities hardly anything at all. But the really interesting thing is not *how much* you gain, but *where* you gain it.

Naturally, being pregnant and all, you'd expect some increase in the size of your tummy. And then there are your boobs. You'll be amazed at how big they get. (But be sure to keep some amazement in reserve for your first week postpartum, when they'll get even bigger.)

But while it's easy to overlook, being both literally and figuratively overshadowed by your belly, there is definite growth in other areas. We're talking about a bigger butt and, shall we say, *sturdier* thighs. There are two reasons for these changes.

Ballast: Your legs need to be bigger and stronger in order to support a substantially heavier torso (that belly and boobs combo).

Maternal fat stores: Whether or not you are planning to breast-feed, your body starts laying down fat stores, preparing you to nourish your new baby.

The bottom line is that being pregnant means gaining weight, and usually all over. Comfort yourself with the fact that by and large it's good fat, designed to support your pregnancy. So go ahead, have that second brownie. Your baby (if not your butt) will thank you for it in the end.

CHARDONNAY CLARIFYING MASK

Overnight mask for oily skin

If you're missing your nightly glass of Chardonnay now that you're pregnant, then this wonderfully simple mask will go a little way to remind you of the heady days of summer. Wine tasting in a sun-drenched valley. Picnicking by the side of the river. Relaxing with your honey under the stars. (Delightful occasions, I feel obliged to tell you, that take on a whole new level of nostalgia when you have children.)

Moving on, the egg whites also pack a punch. They're great for oily skin, as they help draw out impurities. While this mask will tighten a little over your skin, it's cool and comfortable enough to keep on your face for hours at a time.

Please note: Don't even think about tasting this mask. Raw egg whites aren't a good idea for pregnant women.

Makes 1 application
1 egg white
1 tablespoon white wine

In a small bowl, whisk the egg white and wine into a froth and spread onto your face. You can keep this mask on all night and then rinse off with lukewarm water in the morning.

C YOU LATER, ACNE

A wake-up call for unruly skin

Even if you had perfect, blemish-free skin as a teenager, those pregnancy hormones can still do a number on your face. Fortunately, this fresh and fruity vitamin C–enriched astringent tonic can zap even the most persistent pimples. After you've extracted the juice from half of a grapefruit for this recipe, broil the other half under the grill for a few minutes and then drizzle with a little honey for a sweet and tart breakfast treat. That way, you'll be enjoying the powerful antioxidant properties of the grapefruit's vitamin C, inside and out.

Makes about 7 applications

1 tablespoon fresh grapefruit juice
1½ tablespoons witch hazel
½ tablespoon rubbing alcohol

In a small, clean jar with a lid, combine all the ingredients and shake to blend. Apply the tonic to your face with a cotton ball, using upward strokes. This recipe makes enough for about a week assuming 1 application per day, but you may find that your skin clears up in just a few days. Store the tonic in the refrigerator.

BUDDHA BELLY MASK
Soothe your growing belly

Snacking fifteen times a day? You might as well feed your belly from the outside, too. As your midsection stretches to places you never thought possible, make time to show your appreciation for your baby's temporary home by liberally applying this delicious moisturizing mask made of avocado, honey, and molasses to your belly. When you rinse clean after applying the mask, you'll also be gently exfoliating the skin. While this mask looks and smells delicious, please don't be tempted to taste it, as it contains essential oil.

If you need to buy molasses to make the belly mask, opt for blackstrap molasses. It's an excellent source of iron and calcium, essential nutrients for a pregnant woman, and is also rich in copper, manganese, potassium, and magnesium. You may not want to sweeten your tea with it, but it certainly makes gingerbread delicious.

Makes 1 application

¼ cup avocado
2 tablespoons fresh orange juice
2 teaspoons molasses
5 drops chamomile essential oil

In a small bowl, mash the avocado, then stir in the remaining ingredients. Add extra orange juice if the mixture is too thick. Spread the mask over your belly and leave it on for at least 30 minutes before using a warm washcloth to rinse it off.

TOO MUCH BABY, NOT ENOUGH LUNG

How to cope with compromised breathing

Along with pretty much everything else in your body, your respiratory system undergoes some major changes when you're pregnant. In fact, you become super efficient at breathing, inhaling, and exhaling more than the average nonpregnant person does.

Despite this, you may find yourself increasingly short of breath as your pregnancy progresses. Not content with relying on you for every last nutrient, your fetus is now taking up residence in your abdominal cavity, displacing some fairly important organs (like your lungs).

While you may think you've been breathing pretty successfully for a number of years now, pregnancy is a good time to improve your technique. Learning how to breathe deeply from your diaphragm promotes relaxation and relieves the strain in the neck, chest, and upper back that comes from breathing incorrectly.

At the risk of seeming hokey, this simple visualization can help. Sit in a comfortable position and close your eyes. Slowly inhale a deep breath. Imagine that this breath is giving your baby-to-be a big bear hug. Exhale, and imagine the hug slowly releasing your baby. Repeat until you feel as though you are surrounding your baby with your breath, gently touching and hugging his or her entire body.

Not big on visualization exercises? Try sleeping semi-propped-up on pillows instead. Or for a temporary fix at a moment of particular breathlessness, raise your arms over your head and breathe deeply (this will lift your ribcage off your baby). As a general rule, try to take long, slow breaths. And most importantly, relax.

SALMON WITH LEMON PESTO

A healthy feast for you and your baby

By the second trimester, it's likely that your morning sickness has subsided and you now find yourself hungry all the time. Constantly, ravenously, indiscriminately hungry. While it's tempting to eat any and all things that loom on your horizon, a little discretion now will pay dividends later on. This salmon dish is low in fat, high in protein, and just bursting with the essential fatty acids that help your baby grow healthy brain and skin cells. As an added bonus, the lemon zest can alleviate your old friend constipation, and the new bane of your life, water retention.

Makes 2 servings
2 salmon fillets

Lemon Pesto:
2 tablespoons olive oil
1 tablespoon grated lemon zest
$1/2$ teaspoon garlic-lemon salt
1 tablespoon grated Parmesan cheese
$1/2$ tablespoon pine nuts
$1/2$ teaspoon sugar, honey, or maple syrup

Preheat the oven to 375°F. Pat the salmon fillets dry and set aside.

　　To make the pesto: In a blender, combine all the ingredients. Blend to a smooth sauce. Place the salmon fillets in an oiled ovenproof glass pan. Spread the pesto over the fillets. Refrigerate, marinating for 30 minutes. Bake in the oven for 15 to 20 minutes, or until firm. Brush the salmon with any leftover pesto before serving.

ICED BERRY LEMONADE
A nutrient-packed zinger

Is there any fruit more efficient than the humble raspberry? So small, yet crammed with powerful properties, both antioxidant (protecting the body's tissues from oxygen-related damage) and antimicrobial (helping prevent yeast infections). Raspberries also contain folic acid and vitamins B$_6$ and C, and research suggests that they provide cancer-fighting nutrients, too. All of which may explain why this delicious all-natural lemonade packs quite a punch.

Makes 2 servings

$1/2$ cup fresh lemon juice
$1/4$ cup honey
2 decaffeinated tea bags
$1/2$ cup blueberries
$1/2$ cup raspberries
3 cups water

In a small saucepan, combine the lemon juice and honey. Cook over low heat just until the honey has melted. Remove from the heat, add the tea bags, and let steep for 3 to 5 minutes. Remove the tea bags. In a blender, combine the tea mixture, blueberries, and raspberries. With the machine running, gradually add the water to make a smooth mixture. Chill thoroughly and serve over ice, or refrigerate for up to 1 week.

AVOIDING STRETCH MARKS
You can run, but you can't hide

While you're probably enjoying your growing belly and are amazed by your expanding boobs, there's little to like about the stretch marks that tend to appear during the second trimester.

Officially, stretch marks go by the sinister-sounding name of *striae gravidarum*. Around 90 percent of all pregnant women will be horrified to find them on their abdomen, buttocks, thighs, and breasts.

As you get bigger, the middle layer of skin, the dermis, becomes unusually stretched (along with your capacity for sleep, and tolerance for people who take more than thirty seconds at the ATM). This puts your skin's collagen under strain. Weakened, it may tear, and bingo, there's a stretch mark.

If your mother got stretch marks, then you probably will too, although you won't know for sure until it's too late. So, if you're not a gambling woman, you may want to try one or all of the tactics below. None are actually scientifically proven to help, but they *may*. And that's good enough for me.

Drink more water: Well-hydrated skin stretches better.
Use a loofah: Gently massaging the susceptible areas improves circulation, which may help.
Gain weight slowly and steadily: Rapid and/or excessive weight gain can make stretch marks worse.
Apply cream daily: Some women say that simple cocoa butter works wonders. Of course, they may be the same women who don't get stretch marks anyway. (Their babies are probably ugly, too.)

STAYING FIT IN THE SECOND TRIMESTER

Enjoying your new-found energy

By the second trimester, your energy level may have returned to normal, or even exceeded it. Capitalize on this now (because it won't last) by taking some gentle exercise. Here's what's suitable and safe for pregnant women.

Prenatal fitness class: Working out in a group setting will also afford you the opportunity to pick out your child's future playmates while they're still in utero.

Swimming: This is pretty much the perfect exercise for pregnant women. You're considerably more buoyant than usual, and it's easy on the joints. Plus, swimming is a great way to relate to your unborn baby, as you both glide around in a pool of warm water.

Yoga: Under the supervision of a qualified practitioner, prenatal yoga can enhance your flexibility and improve your ability to relax (both pretty useful talents come delivery day).

Kegel exercises: Keep doing them. While not exactly a full-body workout, you'll be glad you stuck with the program, especially when you learn that they may also ease perineal pain after the birth and help you avoid stress incontinence later in life. Work up to 50 repetitions 4 times a day, and hold each contraction for 10 seconds.

But however much energy you think you have, please refrain from the following activities:

Tennis, running: During pregnancy, the hormone progesterone causes many joints and ligaments to loosen. To stay clear of injuries, try to avoid any activity that involves jerky movements.

Skydiving, downhill skiing, white-water rafting, pro football: At this stage, your baby is no longer safely protected by your pelvis, so please steer clear of exercises (and contact sports) that could result in abdominal trauma.

Remember, however you choose to exercise, always *stay well hydrated and avoid becoming overheated or fatigued.*

IT'S A REVELATION
Get behind the mask of pregnancy

Everybody talks about the glow of pregnancy, and I'm sure some women do feel radiant. The rest of us find ourselves dealing with the many and varied side effects of impending motherhood, not least of which is *chloasma*, or facial-skin discoloration (the so-called mask of pregnancy).

A cream that gently exfoliates the skin can be a real help. Try this pumpkin and papaya mixture that works like a scrub without being abrasive to your skin. (Remember, the sun can aggravate skin discoloration, so be sure to apply facial sunblock every day, and especially after using this cream as your skin may be more vulnerable.) Use no more than twice a week.

Makes 2 applications
½ papaya, seeded
1 egg white
15-ounce can pumpkin
1 teaspoon honey

Scoop the flesh from the papaya half and mash it in a bowl. In another bowl, whisk the egg white until frothy. Add the egg white, pumpkin, and honey to the papaya. Stir to mix thoroughly and apply to your face. Leave on for 10 minutes, then rinse off and apply sunblock. Refrigerate for up to 1 week.

ROSEWATER FACIAL COCKTAIL

Clarifying toner for acne-prone skin

There are some ingredients you might expect to see in a skin-care recipe, like the rosewater, lemon juice, and honey in this fabulous toner. But vodka? In fact, the alcohol in vodka is a powerful but natural astringent that can draw out your skin's impurities. And if you're bemoaning your recently curtailed once-extravagant social life, then at least you can think of it as a cocktail for your face.

Makes about 7 applications

1/2 tablespoon honey
1/2 teaspoon fresh lemon juice
1/2 tablespoon rosewater
1 tablespoon vodka

In a clean jar with a lid, combine the ingredients and shake to blend. To use, cleanse your face and then apply the toner with a cotton ball. Cover and refrigerate the toner, and use within 1 week.

THE THIRD TRIMESTER

Congratulations. You're huge.

Maternity clothes simply don't fit anymore. You think you need a pedicure and bikini wax, but you couldn't say for sure. And your belly now precedes you into the room, with the rest of you following on a few seconds later (your butt a few seconds after that, if you've really been pounding the Ben & Jerry's).

It's lucky, then, that you're in the homestretch. There are only three short months until your baby makes his or her grand entrance, which really (and maybe more importantly) means that you have only a few weeks in which to pamper yourself in glorious and peaceful solitude.

So, as your ankles swell and your appetite shrinks, make the most of the opportunity to enjoy some leisurely spa treatments in the comfort of your own home. But don't delay. Soon enough, *leisurely* will be a concept as foreign to you as *breakfast in bed* or *dinner and a movie*. Soon you will have an actual baby on your hands, a baby who for one reason (hungry) or another (cranky) may not share your views on the absolute necessity of restorative massages and rejuvenating facials.

STRAWBERRY SMOOTHIE
A protein-packed fruit punch

The blender is possibly the greatest invention known to the pregnant woman. At this stage in the gestation of your child, you are probably more tired than you could ever have imagined (though you ain't seen nothin' yet). If you have only enough energy to throw a few ingredients into a blender and press a switch, then this protein- and nutrient-filled concoction is perfect for you.

For the scientists among you, blue-green algae powder (also known as spirulina) is 60 percent vegetable protein, and is high in antioxidants, iron, and vitamins B_6 and B_{12}. It's also a rich source of GLA, an essential amino acid found in breast milk. Look for it at your local natural-foods store.

Makes 1 serving
1 cup milk
1 cup fresh or frozen strawberries
1 tablespoon blue-green algae powder (spirulina)
$1/4$ teaspoon vitamin C powder
1 tablespoon flaxseed oil
1 tablespoon protein powder

In a blender, whiz all the ingredients together until thoroughly combined. Enjoy immediately.

BAREFOOT & PREGNANT BELLY CAST

Preserve your belly in all its glory

While taking a belly cast requires a little effort, some patience, and a pretty big sense of humor, you will end up with something that can only be described as a work of art. Mount it on the wall for all to enjoy, or (if you'd rather not have such a visible reminder of your girth) simply invert it and use as a fruit bowl or a bed for the dog.

You will need:
A disposable drop cloth
Scissors
3 to 4 rolls of fast-setting plaster tape
(such as M-Pact), 4 inches wide and 5 yards long
Olive oil as needed
At least 1 helper

Cover the floor with a drop cloth. Cut the rolls of plaster tape into 18-inch strips, and fill a basin with warm water. Wearing just underwear that you don't mind throwing away, sit on a chair so that you create a soft angle between your thighs and torso. To avoid the cast sticking to you (ouch), generously slather your upper body with oil, including the shoulders, the tops of the thighs, and around the sides of the torso.

Have your helper hold a strip of plaster tape at each end and slide it through the water for a few seconds. Holding the strip taut, firmly place it on the belly. Repeat, using a second strip, slightly overlapping the first. When you have a few in place, use a finger to smooth the plaster. Continue until you have at least 2 layers of plaster strips on your entire torso. Be sure to cover the tops of the thighs and the breasts to help define the shape of your belly. Ten minutes after completing the last layer, hold the sides of the belly cast as you carefully wiggle out. Handle the cast with care until it is completely dry (in about 48 hours). Then cut and shape any rough edges, and behold: It's your belly, preserved for posterity.

SMART SLEEPING POSITIONS
How to get a good night's rest (before it's too late)

In what seems like a cruel twist of fate, the more tired you become (because you're pregnant), the harder it is to sleep (because you're pregnant). Along with heartburn, backache, frequent bathroom breaks, and imminent-parenthood anxiety, a huge belly is simply not conducive to a good night's rest.

But rest you should. Before too long, you'll be measuring shut-eye in terms of minutes rather than hours. So, force yourself to sleep as much as you can now. Go to bed early and sleep late. Drink hot milk, listen to soothing music, read a really boring novel. And most importantly, find a comfortable position.

On your back: The books (including this one) say that sleeping on your left side is best because you avoid squishing major blood vessels, compromising your baby's oxygen supply. In reality, if your doctor hasn't suggested that you might be a candidate for such an eventuality (if, for example, you have placental problems), you probably needn't worry. And even if you always seem to wake on your back, it's unlikely you've been there all night (seeing as you're getting up to pee every hour).

On your stomach: While it won't harm your baby, lying on your belly at this point in your pregnancy is probably well-nigh impossible, so let's move on.

On your side: For many pregnant women, lying on the side with knees bent is the most comfortable way to sleep. Support your upper leg by putting a pillow between your knees. If your back aches, try one under your abdomen. You can also buy a full-body pillow that conforms supportively to your fulsome shape.

RISE AND SHINE

Oatmeal mask for dry skin

Pregnancy is one of the few times when you're actually encouraged to indulge, which is probably why so many women have more than one child. But, as you may have noticed, being pregnant isn't all about you. You have your unborn child to consider. It's good to know then, that when you pamper yourself, you're actually helping to create a stress-free environment for your growing baby. Start a relaxing day by treating yourself to this incredibly soothing facial mask designed to help dry skin feel baby soft.

Makes 1 application

1 cup rolled oats
2 tablespoons powdered milk
About 1 tablespoon water, as needed
2 or 3 gauze squares
1 rubber band

In a food processor, process the oats to a fine powder. Put the oat powder in a bowl and add the powdered milk. Gradually stir in water until the mask reaches a creamy consistency. Unfold the gauze squares and position them on the skin of your face, leaving your eyes, nostrils, and mouth exposed. Generously apply all of the oatmeal mask on top of the gauze, taking care to lap it over the edges of the gauze so that the mask sticks to your face. (While you can apply this mask directly to your face, the gauze makes it easier to remove.)

Draw a hot bath (not too hot!) while you are waiting; the steam will enhance the effects of the mask. After 15 minutes, remove the mask by lifting up and removing the squares of gauze. Fold them so that the oatmeal is contained, seal with the rubber band, and drop into the bath for an all-over skin-softening effect.

STAYING FIT IN THE THIRD TRIMESTER

The great pregnancy balancing act

By this stage, you're so perpetually exhausted that the very idea of exercising would make you laugh if only you had the lung capacity. If you've been following an exercise program throughout your pregnancy, however, there's no reason why you shouldn't keep on track. Just keep a few simple precautions in mind.

Balance: Basically, you don't have much of it. By this point in your pregnancy, your center of gravity has shifted dramatically; unfortunately, your mental perception of how to stay balanced may lag far behind the physical reality. Please be aware of this when in the upright position.

Exercising on your back: Lying on your back when heavily pregnant is not medically recommended, as it puts the entire weight of your belly on the vein that carries blood from the lower body back to the heart (which can quickly lower your blood pressure). Also, you should never, ever do sit-ups when pregnant (or at any other time, really).

Kegels: By now you may be so big that Kegel exercises are the only physical activity that you can accomplish without feeling breathless. That's O.K. Just focus all your efforts on your pelvic floor and comfort yourself with the knowledge that while you may have gained fifty pounds and doubled the circumference of each thigh, your pelvic floor has never been in better shape.

And once again, whatever kind of exercise you do (or don't do), remember to *stay well hydrated and avoid becoming overheated or fatigued.*

FRESH AND FRUITY

Citrus mask for oily skin

Think you know how your skin behaves? Sadly, all bets are off when you're pregnant. Every day brings something new: pimples, oily patches, irritated areas. It's all down to those raging hormones, the amount of which actually doubles during pregnancy. And this creates all types of interesting conditions. Many moms-to-be become newly acquainted with oily skin. If that's you, try this citrus mask twice a week to unclog pores and tighten the skin.

Makes 2 applications

½ grapefruit, peeled, seeded, and
chopped
1 teaspoon fresh lemon juice
½ apple, peeled, seeded, and
chopped
2 egg whites
35 seedless grapes

In a blender, combine all the ingredients and purée to a smooth paste. Spread half of the mixture evenly over your face and leave for 15 minutes. Remove gently with a warm washcloth. Store the remainder in the fridge, and be sure to use within 1 week.

ASIAN CABBAGE CRUNCH SALAD

The healthiest way to get your greens

Cabbage not in your top-ten list of vegetables? Try this fabulous salad and you'll become a fan. Savoy cabbage helps with constipation, which you may be suffering from, as your digestive system slows down while your pregnancy progresses. The mint balances the acid in your stomach, relieving heartburn, and the almonds help calm your nerves (if, by chance, you're nervous about something). And kelp is pretty much a wonder food. It's high in calcium, iron, and protein —all things a very pregnant lady like yourself needs lots of.

Makes 4 servings

Dressing:
3 tablespoons brown rice vinegar
Juice of 1 lemon
$1/4$ teaspoon salt
$1/4$ teaspoon kelp flakes
3 tablespoons Asian (toasted) sesame oil

2 cups shredded red cabbage
2 cups shredded savoy cabbage
1 cup shredded napa cabbage
$1/4$ cup chopped green onions
$1/4$ cup chopped fresh cilantro
$1/4$ cup chopped fresh mint
$1/4$ cup almonds, toasted (see note) and chopped

To make the dressing: In a small bowl, combine the vinegar, lemon juice, salt, and kelp flakes. Gradually whisk in the oil. Taste and adjust the seasoning. Use now, or cover and refrigerate for up to 1 week.

In a medium bowl, mix the shredded cabbages together. Add dressing to taste and toss well. Finally, add the green onions, cilantro, mint, and almonds and toss again. Dressed, the salad will keep in the refrigerator for 2 to 3 days. Alternatively, toss together all the salad ingredients and leave undressed until serving; the undressed salad with keep, refrigerated, for up to 1 week.

Note: To toast almonds, preheat oven to 350°F. Spread the almonds on a baking sheet and toast for 5 to 10 minutes, until lightly browned.

You may have noticed that, as we've progressed through this book, more and more of our exercises and massages require the assistance of another person. There are two reasons for this. First (at the risk of stating the obvious), you've simply got more pregnant and are therefore more unwieldy and more easily fatigued. You just can't do these activities by yourself. And even if you could, you'd probably overbalance, and I don't want that on my conscience.

Second (and perhaps more important, as the focus of this book is prenatal pampering), these exercises give you an ideal excuse to let someone else do all the hard work while you enjoy a little snooze.

Returning to the task in hand, *counterpressure* (the applying of firm and direct pressure on areas of pain) can be a great way to soothe your aching back. This massage uses small frozen-juice cans, which are just the right size, shape, and temperature to provide relief. In addition to the 2 cans, you'll need 2 athletic socks and a helpful assistant.

Prepare by putting each juice can in a sock. Then, sit facing the back of a regular dining table chair. Squeeze a pillow or two between you and the back of the chair. Have your helper slowly roll the besocked juice cans down your back on either side of the spine, paying particular attention to the mid- to low back, the high hip area, and the part of your buttocks closest to your sacrum.

It feels really, really good. So good that you may want to have someone replicate the technique if you find yourself with back labor a few weeks from now.

YOGA FOR THE THIRD TRIMESTER

Deep squatting, or the Garland

On the list of all-time unappealing childbirth-related words and phrases, *deep squatting* is surely up there, alongside *cracked nipples* and *painful hemorrhoids*. In its own defense, however, squatting is actually the most natural birthing position there is, and the one that most laboring women gravitate to if left to their own devices. Still, if you're of a sensitive nature, you'll be glad to learn that this pose is also known as the Garland. Either way, it's great for opening the hips, strengthening the legs, and improving balance and concentration. Learn how to breathe evenly while holding this position for a minute or so, and you'll be in fine shape to deal with those pesky contractions.

1. Stand up straight, with your back against a wall, feet hip-width apart.

2. With your heels turned in and your toes turned out, inhale as you raise your arms.

3. As you exhale, gently lower yourself down into a squatting position. Bring your hands together in a prayer position.

4. Press down on the insides of your knees with your elbows. Use this pressure to open up your hips and thighs, deepening the stretch in the hips.

5. Lengthen your spine as much as possible by tucking your tailbone down, lifting your sternum up, and rolling your shoulders down and back.

To make things more challenging, get into the same starting position, but don't lower your body all the way down. Instead, stand with your legs wide apart in a high squat. Soften your upper body, and let your lower body do all the work. Tuck your tailbone in to keep your spine nice and straight. Go down as far as you comfortably can, bearing in mind that you'll have to stand up again at some point.

Hold either pose for up to 90 seconds.

HAND 'EM OVER

Be kind to your carpal tunnel

Even if you're not a professional concert pianist, you may find that you've recently developed painful carpal tunnel syndrome in one or both wrists. This is yet another by-product of baby making and is caused by those extra fluids of yours exerting pressure on the nerve in your wrist.

Fortunately, help is at hand. Actually, at both of them, although you'll need to rope in a willing volunteer.

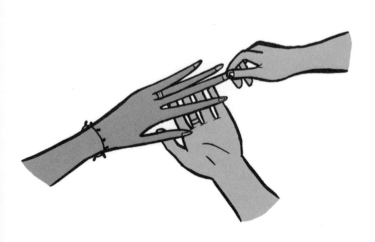

Here's what your helper should do:

Sit next to the mom-to-be. Take mom's hand, palm down, in both of your hands. Using your two thumbs at once, press down the top of her hand from the base of the fingers, past the wrist joint a few inches, and into the valley between the two bones of the lower arm. Do this several times, starting with a different finger each time.

Then, hold her wrist with one hand, and with the other grab one of her fingers at the base. Twist it back and forth while moving upward. At her fingertip, give a little pinch. Work on all five fingers in this way.

Finally, turn her hand over so her palm is up. Lace your little fingers into the spaces on either side of her middle finger, letting your other fingers fit comfortably between her other fingers. (Your fingers should be cupping the back of her hand, with your thumbs hovering over her palm.) Use alternate thumbs to draw circles all over the palm, massaging from the crease of her wrist down to the webs between the fingers.

FRESH CHEEKS TONER
For a calming effect

Some pregnant women suffer from acne, waking up to a new crop of pimples every morning. Others get patches of dry, irritated skin. So much for the highly touted glow of pregnancy.

Whatever's happening to your skin right now, you can pretty much bet that it's all due to hormonal changes. While you may just have to wait until you have a baby in your arms before your skin reverts back to its normal type, using this toner after cleansing your face can help restore its natural acid/alkali balance. You'll find witch hazel, rosewater, and glycerin at your local health-food store or drugstore.

Makes 7 applications
1 tablespoon apple juice
1 tablespoon witch hazel
1 tablespoon rosewater
½ tablespoon glycerin

In a small bowl, combine all the ingredients and stir to blend. After cleansing your face, saturate a cotton ball with the toner and dab away any remaining traces of dirt or oil. This recipe makes a week's worth. Store the remaining toner in a clean, airtight jar in the refrigerator, and discard anything that remains after 1 week.

COPING WITH CANKLES

When it's not just your belly that's getting bigger

For the uninitiated (you first- and second-trimester gals), the *cankle* is the part of your body that looks like your calf, but is where your ankle used to be.

This alarming and frankly unsightly physiological change is due to edema, or fluid retention. By the end of your pregnancy, you could be carrying around an extra twenty pounds or so of fluid, and thanks to gravity and your slower circulation, it tends to settle in your legs, feet, and hands.

Here's what you can do about it.

To reduce swelling in your feet: Lie on the floor with your feet up on the couch. Make lazy circles with your feet to help your muscles circulate your blood and lymph (the fluid that's causing the swelling). If the thought of (a) lowering your cumbersome body onto the floor, or (b) hauling it up again, sounds laughably impossible, even sitting with your feet on an ottoman can help.

To reduce swelling in your hands: Raise your arms above your head and make slow circles at the wrist, alternating directions. When you feel like you can't do any more, lay your forearms across the top of your head and rest for a few breaths. Then, bring your arms down in front of you, palms facing up. Slide the inside edge of your left forearm along your right arm, from the crease of your wrist to the elbow, and then from elbow to shoulder. Repeat with your right arm.

SIMPLY SCIATIC

Quick relief for a pain in the butt

The sciatic pain that began in your second trimester as the occasional twinge may now be causing you serious agony in your lower back, buttocks, and legs. But there's no need to suffer in silence. Holler for a friend and show them this page.

Here's what your accomplice should do.

Double-hip squeeze: Ask the pregnant person to sit backward in an armless chair, a pillow or two at her front. Make a fist with each of your hands and push them into the meat of her butt cheeks. (Imagine that you're pushing your fists toward each other.) Press as hard and for as long as the mom-to-be wants (which will probably be harder and longer than you have strength for). Then, twist your fists all over the butt muscles and hips.

Finally, push the knuckles closest to the top of your hand down from just under the ridge of her hipbone into the butt area. Repeat several times, taking care not to push right on the bone.

Mom-to-be, you're on your own for the next one (your friend having beat a hasty retreat after all that butt pushing).

Sacral scrub: Put the thumb and index finger edge of your fist flat against your sacrum (the triangular bone at the base of your spine), and make a circular scrubbing motion all over the top and borders of the bone. Then, use the flat part of your index finger knuckle to saw back and forth along its angular borders. If you find any spots that trigger sudden sciatic pain, use the pointy part of your knuckle to apply pressure until the tenderness dissipates (this may take up to 2 minutes).

SWEET POTATO POTION

Intense nighttime moisturizing for oil-prone skin

The sweet potato: Nutritionally sound (it's a good source of vitamins C and B$_6$, folic acid, and potassium). Great in soups and pies. A staple on the Thanksgiving table. And now you can even use it on your face. This rich but light night cream is designed to help balance oil-prone skin gently but effectively. Plus, as sweet potatoes contain the antioxidant beta carotene, using it regularly may even slow the aging process.

Makes about 3 applications

½ teaspoon almond oil
½ teaspoon glycerin
½ baked sweet potato
1 tablespoon whole-milk yogurt

In a medium bowl, combine the almond oil and glycerin. Scoop out the flesh of the baked sweet potato half and add it to the almond oil mixture. Stir in the yogurt until smooth. Spread the mixture on your face and leave overnight. Keep leftover cream in a clean jar in the refrigerator for up to 2 days.

PERINEAL MASSAGE
Make room for baby

Not the kind of massage you'll find in your average spa, perineal massage is reputed to help to stretch the vaginal tissues the same way that your baby's head will during birth, only in a gentler and more controlled way.

With clean hands, short thumbnails (very important), and a lot of water-soluble lubricant, sit in a comfy position with your legs apart. Insert your thumbs into your vagina, pressing downward and to the sides, and gently stretch this opening until you feel a slight burning sensation. Hold this position for a couple of minutes. Then, gently massage the lower half of the vagina, pulling outward and forward as you do so. Those in the know recommend that you start perineal massage at week 34, and do it daily, for 3 or 4 minutes at a time.

Experts aside, there is clearly a big difference in size between your two thumbs and a baby's head, but anything that claims to reduce tearing or the need for an episiotomy has to be worth a try. In practice, however, I think you'll find reaching over your eight-months-plus pregnant belly and down toward your nether regions requires unnaturally long arms. The good news is it doesn't have to be *you* doing the massaging. This is a great opportunity for your significant other to realize once and for all that now children are in the picture, your intimate life will never, ever be the same again. But remember, if you start enjoying perineal massage, somebody's thumbs are in the wrong place.

BABY SHOWER ETIQUETTE FOR THE MOM-TO-BE

Or, how to get what you really want

Did you know that in some countries, pregnant women don't get baby showers? Crazy, huh? One of the great things about being pregnant (some would say the main reason for getting pregnant in the first place) is the loot. Here are some slightly devious (but perfectly acceptable) strategies to guarantee you'll get the good stuff.

Enlist a friend's help: It's technically bad form to throw your own shower, but there's no law against asking a friend to host one for you. Choose somebody who's known for her fabulous parties.

Register: You may be uncomfortable with registering for baby gifts, but you'll wish you had when the first three boxes you open each contain a diaper bag (the undisputed toaster of the baby-shower world).

Make it easy for people: Register online. Those friends who still have social lives and would rather spend their lunch hour lunching than picking out onesies will thank you.

Keep gift receipts: Almost anything can be returned. Just be sure you can dredge up a good reason why your best friend will never see your baby wearing the dry-clean-only white-linen button-down shirt she picked out.

Have a girl: Everyone knows that the shopping is so much better for girl babies. Go into any baby store and you'll see that a good three-quarters of the floor space is devoted to pretty and pink, with clothes so fashionable you'll wish *you* weighed between 7 and 12 pounds.

But whoever hosts your shower, and whatever wonderful gifts you get, don't forget to ask a responsible friend to help you keep track of who gave what while you're opening the boxes. This will allow you to write thank-you cards that are both timely and personal (because it's never too early to set a good example for your fetus).

YOUR IN-HOME FULL-BODY MASSAGE

Down with fatigue, up with energy

While it's always nice to go to a real spa for a massage (the soft, soothing music, the free herbal tea and orange slices), it's eminently possible to replicate the entire experience in the comfort of your own home, especially if you have a willing volunteer.

Choose someone with both the energy and the patience to practice *effleurage*, the long gliding strokes used by professional massage therapists, which increase the efficiency of the circulatory system and the removal of waste products from your body's tissues. This technique, done well, can really stimulate lymphatic drainage, giving you renewed energy and vitality.

Here's what you have to do (the easy bit): Lie on your left side. You need 3 pillows: one to support your neck, one for hugging, and one for under the bent knee of your top (right) leg.

Here's what your sister/friend/partner has to do (slightly more complicated but ultimately an act of kindness to a very pregnant women): Using plenty of lotion, hold the inside of the bent knee with one hand while gliding up the thigh with the other. Be sure to work up into the gluteal area, and up and over the top of the thighbone. Remember to use firm pressure, as your intention is to move fluid. Always focus pressure toward the torso (the hand should just lightly drag on the return trip).

Use the same action on the lower leg, massaging from ankle to knee, on the upper arm (elbow to shoulder) and lower arm (wrist to elbow). Repeat before gently waking up the mom-to-be and asking her to switch sides.

WHAT TO TAKE TO THE HOSPITAL

Staying cute while contracting

There's absolutely no reason why a little thing like childbirth
should put a cramp in your personal style, as long as you pack
your hospital bag with a bit of care and a lot of makeup. So
while the scented candles and soothing CDs may be helpful,
read the following for what tops my list of birthing necessities.

Lip gloss: Or, at the very least, a tinted lip balm. Having a baby is a challenging way to pass a day or two, and you'll likely become pretty dehydrated if you're in a hospital that chooses (bizarrely) not to let its laboring moms-to-be drink water. Be sure to bring something that you can slather on your cracked and chapped lips.

Body lotion: Pack one that smells the same as your favorite perfume. It'll conjure up all kinds of good memories and positive associations, thus distracting you from your current level of discomfort/pain/agony. Your partner can use it as a massage lotion; you can use it as hand cream.

Cosmetics: A lick of mascara goes a long way to make you look fresh and wide awake (as opposed to haggard and exhausted).

Going-home outfit: Oddly enough, having a baby doesn't necessarily mean losing the belly. So while your newborn will leave the hospital looking quite fabulous, you'll be wearing an outfit pretty similar to what you wore when you arrived two days before. Which is why now is the time to start dropping hints for a little something that's guaranteed to fit perfectly right after the birth. I refer, of course, to jewelry.

NOW YOU ARE TWO

Congratulations. You have a baby.

You are without doubt the cleverest, most resourceful, most amazing woman in the world.

Now the fun really starts. The first three months after the birth of your baby are generally agreed to be a time of enormous change, requiring rapid adjustment. While your baby gets comfortable in the outside world, dealing with such pressing issues as eating, sleeping, and pooping, you spend your waking hours (of which there are many) wondering if you'll ever get a good night's sleep again (you won't), why your skin is breaking out again (it's hormonal), and why, if your newborn weighs just 7 pounds, your shoulders ache as if you've got a 15-pound bowling ball strapped to your chest.

Now, more than ever, the spa that is your bathroom/bedroom/kitchen will be your sanctuary. And while your baby hollers and the dirty laundry overflows and the cupboards grow increasingly bare, take my advice and take a little time for yourself.

During the weeks and months that follow the birth, do whatever you need to do (be it massage or mask, hot scented bath, or ice-cold beverage of choice) to make yourself feel a little more relaxed, a little less stressed, and altogether a little more human. Your baby will thank you. And mothers everywhere will salute you.

YUMMY PEC STRETCH
Work a little muscle-strain magic

If your baby is an average newborn (in an exceptionally intelligent and amazingly beautiful way, of course), then he or she probably loves to be held. For hours and hours and hours at a time.

This is not a bad thing, as keeping your baby close really helps the bonding process. However, because of the way you are most likely holding your baby (with your shoulders folded inward and your head tilted to one side and down as you gaze adoringly at that fuzzy little head), along with the increased weight of your breasts (I told you they'd get bigger), the pectoral muscles at the front of your shoulders will be feeling the strain. The energizing stretch below can help.

1. With your arms extended, hold a belt or rope at shoulder height. Your forearms should be facing and parallel to the floor, with your hands 6 to 12 inches farther apart than your shoulders.

2. Take a deep breath, and as you exhale move the belt over your head and behind you so that your forearms are facing the ceiling. Keep your arms straight and your shoulders down. Try not to jut your head or back forward.

3. Take 3 full breaths in this position, while squeezing your shoulder blades together. On the fourth breath, return to your starting position.

LOOKING GOOD FOR THE FIRST PHOTOS
(Even though you were in labor for thirty-six hours)

Look at any photo of a first-time mom just hours after the delivery and you'll be horrified. No woman could possibly look more tired, more haggard, and more annoyed to be viewed through a lens. But look at the same woman after the birth of her second child, and you'll be amazed. How fresh she looks, how radiant, how happy. How unbelievable.

Now, a lot of that has to do with the fact that second time around, the birth and first few weeks simply aren't quite as challenging as they are with the first. With the second, you know what you're doing. You know that you're going to be exhausted beyond belief, but that sooner or later, you and your little one will find a comfortable, mutually beneficial rhythm. You know that breast-feeding is going to hurt like crazy at first, but that it will get better. You know that whatever happens, you'll get through it, *because you already have*.

With that in mind, here's what the second-time mom knows about the immediate post-birth photo-session (and now you do, too).

Wear makeup: Lipstick, powder, even a bit of mascara if you can steady your hand long enough. You'll be glad you made the effort. Really, really glad.

Don't wear your hospital-issue gown: Take your own pajamas to the hospital, or change into some cute sweats.

Stand up (if you can): Nobody looks very glamorous tucked into a hospital bed.

And most of all, pretend this is your second baby: That way, you'll project the relaxed and confident air of one who knows everything there is to know about babies.

MOTHER'S LITTLE HELPER

Soothing shoulder, neck, and head massage

This thorough massage promotes relaxation, releases tension, and helps your body deal with the new physical challenges associated with a small child (and the heavy equipment that comes with it).

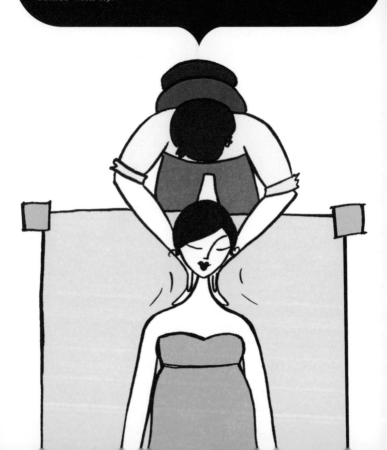

Lie face up on your bed so that your head is at the edge. Get a friend to sit on a chair placed behind your head, with body lotion and these instructions in hand.

Here's what your helper should do.

Shoulder: Start with both hands at mom's breastbone. Sweep across her chest to the shoulders, pump down at the top of the arms, and sweep back under the top of the shoulders and up the neck. Then squeeze the flesh of her upper shoulder from the neck out to the shoulder. Finally, gently push her shoulders down toward her toes. Hold for up to a minute and release slowly.

Neck: Start by gently turning her head to one side. Glide your fingers down the back of her neck from the skull to the base of the neck and up again. Then, using the flat part of your knuckles, massage from the base of her skull, down the neck, and along the top of her shoulder. Turn your wrist and repeat in reverse.

Head: Start by asking mom to let her head hang heavy as you hold it securely in your hands. Slowly lift her head, moving her chin toward her chest as far as comfort allows. Hold her head with one hand and use the other to draw up one side of her neck. Repeat on the other side.

BABY FOOT AND LEG MASSAGE
Pure relaxation for both of you

Technically speaking, this is not a massage for you. But since caressing your new baby's perfect little body is likely to release those feel-good endorphins in your brain, I think it counts as a pampering experience.

Start by making sure your baby is a willing participant. Hold his or her hips and gently sweep down his legs until you reach his feet. As you do so, ask him if he's ready for a massage. If he starts to cry or fuss, you can probably take that as a no, but if he remains calm and seems content, then you have permission to proceed.

With a little organic vegetable oil in your hand, and a naked baby in front of you, work your way through these five steps, first on one side of his body and then the other.

1. Hold your baby's ankle with one hand. Form a C shape with the other and swoop his leg from ankle to hip. Do several passes, switching hands as you do.

2. Place both hands around the top of his thigh. Squeeze and then release. Repeat just above his knee and at his ankle.

3. Holding his foot in both hands, walk your thumbs up the sole from heel to toes. Squeeze each toe and give each a little back-and-forth twist.

4. With your thumbs over the top of his foot, massage from the base of the toes toward the ankle to cover the entire top of the foot.

5. Roll his leg between your hands from the thigh to the ankle. Then hold his leg just behind the knee and gently bounce it.

SLEEPLESS IN [INSERT HOME TOWN HERE]

Survival tactics for the new mom

As if to counterbalance all that big-eyed, sweet-smelling cuteness, babies are also attention-demanding, energy-sapping little monsters. While tiredness is part of the territory for new parents, there are some things you can do to wrest a few extra minutes of sleep from the toothless jaws of your new offspring.

Share a bed with your baby: Co-sleeping is one of those touchy child-rearing subjects that most people have an opinion about, so let's not even get into the *is-it-safe?/will-people-think-I'm-crazy?* debate. The undeniable benefit, if you're breast-feeding, is that you don't have to get out of bed to feed the baby. After a bit of practice, you won't even have to sit up. And a few months down the line, you may find that your baby can latch on and enjoy a full meal without even waking you up.

Sleep when your baby does: Every experienced mom will tell you this is the smart thing to do. And if you're like every new mom, you'll ignore them and use the time to rush around doing pointless things like tidying up. Don't be a martyr. The most active thing you should be doing while your baby naps is dozing off in a nice warm bath.

Share the feeds: Many breastfed babies will take a bottle. Once your milk supply is established, you can start expressing. Pump a bottle in the morning and get dad to give the 5 A.M. feed the following day. This could mean as much as six hours of uninterrupted sleep for you. Of course, you'll have a tired and cranky daddy to deal with, but that's the subject of an entirely different book.

THERE'S A BABY IN YOUR SPA
Why the pampering doesn't have to end

You've worked your way through 40 or so weeks of pregnancy. You've eaten right, exercised some, and tried to live a virtuous and healthy life. And, if you've been adhering to the principles of this book, you've scrubbed, soothed, massaged, and generally relaxed yourself through every single day of it. Now you know how important it is to really nurture yourself, mind and body, when you're doing something as amazing as having a baby. It stands to reason then, that when taking on the even more incredible and consuming job of being a mother, your physical and emotional health deserves even more attention.

Easier said than done, however. Throughout the early days of parenthood, you will believe that responsibility for propelling your new baby into adulthood rests entirely at your door. This is not necessarily the case, as most dads can become quite adept at filling a bottle or finding a diaper and then attaching it to the appropriate part of the baby. Nevertheless, you will probably feel overwhelmed by the never-ending routine of your new life. The feeding, the rocking, the holding, the bathing, the soothing, the feeding. The feeding. The feeding. The feeding.

Because this is what you'll spend most of the first month doing. (That, and peering intently at the contents of every dirty diaper.) Whether they're on the boob or the bottle, most newborns need topping off every three hours. During the average feed, your baby will likely fall asleep, spit up some, dawdle a bit, get gas and need burping, take a little break, poop a couple of times, and dawdle some more, all while taking in a measly few ounces. A single feed seems to take hours, and then, just minutes later, they're hungry all over again. It's completely and utterly exhausting, and you will feel more tired and more desperate for sleep than at any other time in your life.

There is, however, something you can do to give yourself a break. For weeks now, people (friends, relatives, neighbors) have been offering to help. Whether you think they mean it or not is beside the point. This is the time to say yes.

Have them make a meal while you read a trashy magazine, do a load of laundry while you take a nap, or look after the baby while you soak in the tub. At the end of it you'll be more than well informed about celebrity gossip/wearing clean clothes/smelling great. You'll be a happier, more contented, and, dare I say, *better* parent. It's a simple equation. Tense, irritable mom equals fussy, squawking baby. Happy, relaxed mom equals happy, contented baby.

So as you are now officially postpartum (that great and glorious excuse for every misplaced car key and forgotten birthday present), there's every reason the self-pampering should continue. You're doing the most difficult and demanding job in the world (the most exciting and most fulfilling, too). Nurture yourself, and you'll find it easier to nurture your child.

Here endeth the lecture. Now go forth and enjoy your baby. Enjoy your new role as a mom. And enjoy your home spa for as long as there are night creams, facial masks, and body scrubs to be mixed up and relaxed under.

ACKNOWLEDGMENTS

If you've read the introduction (and if not, I encourage you to turn back to the beginning, because it's fascinating stuff), you'll know that I've been fairly busy over the past year or two. Opening and running my spa, Barefoot & Pregnant, as well as being a mom to the demanding but adorable Maxwell and (I hope) a loving and attentive life partner to my incredibly supportive husband, Brad, has taken up most of my time. Which is why I can't take full credit for putting together this little book. Instead, I'd like to thank the following people for making it happen—and happen smoothly:

Lisa Campbell at Chronicle Books, for the opportunity to help even more pregnant women make it to the delivery room feeling pampered and relaxed.

Susan Lawler, for her guidance, support, and friendship throughout the building of my business (and the growing of my fetus).

Kate Hodson, for collaborating on the writing and adding just the right combination of British properness and humor.

Kim Pierce, for her endless research and for keeping me on track both personally and professionally.

And (in no particular order) Heidi Rahlmann Plumb, Angela Weis, Parrish Navarro, Barbara MacMillan, and Dolores Caruthers, my amazing staff of therapists, estheticians, and exercise instructors, for contributing their own remedies, recipes, and years of experience.